Jn 18:2-4
2 Tim 2:13

The Church is the Body of Christ.

Jn 15:1-11
Acts 9:1-6
Rom 12:4-8
1 Cor 12:12-27
Eph 1:22-23
Col 1:18

D0797140

3. The Papacy

The Primacy of Peter

Simon Peter is mentioned by name 195 times in the New Testament. Next comes St. John, who is mentioned just 29 times.

When all twelve Apostles are named, Peter is always listed first; Judas Iscariot is always listed last (Mt 10:2-5; Mk 3:16-19; Lk 6:14-17; and Acts 1:13).

Often: "Peter and the rest of the Apostles" or "Peter and his companions" (Lk 9:32; Mk 16:7; Acts 2:37).

Peter as spokesman for all the Apostles

> Mt 18:21
> Mk 8:29
> Lk 8:45, 12:41
> Jn 6:69

Peter's Primacy

> Mt 16:13-20
> Mt 14:24-33
> Mk 16:7
> Lk 5: Christ preaches to the crowds from
>   *Peter's* fishing boat.
> Lk 22:31-32
> Lk 24:33-35
> Jn 20:6
> Jn 21:15-19
> Acts 1:15-26
> Acts 3:1-9
> Acts 10-11
> Acts 15:6-11
> Gal 1:18

4. Tradition

Mk 7:1-13; Mt 15: 1-9 (Ungodly traditions condemned)

Lk 1:1-4 (Oral tradition came before New Testament Scriptures)

Mk 16:15
Jn 20:30-31
Jn 21:25
1 Cor 11:2
1 Cor 11:23
1 Cor 15:1-2
1 Thess 2:13
2 Thess 2:15
2 Thess 3:6
2 Tim 1:13
2 Tim 2:2
1 Pet 1:25
2 Pet 1:20-21
2 Jn 12
3 Jn 13

5. Scripture vs "*Sola scriptura*" (the Bible Alone)

Authority of the Church

> Deut 17:8-13
> Mt 16:18-19
> Mt 28:19-20
> Lk 10:16
> Acts 15:28-29
> 1 Cor 11:2
> 1 Thess 2:13
> 2 Thess 2:15
> 1 Tim 3:14-15
> 1 Pet 3:15-17
> 2 Pet 1:20-21, 2:1
> 2 Pet 5:1-5

6. "Word of God" Does Not Always Mean "The Bible"

> Is 55:10-11
> Lk 3:2-3
> Lk 4:42-5:1
> Lk 8:11-15
> Jn 1:1, 14
> Acts 4:31

1 Thess 2:13
Heb 4:12-13
Heb 11:3

7. Apostolic Succession

Acts 1:15-26
Acts 14:23
Acts 20:28
1 Cor 12:27-31
Eph 4:11
Eph 2:19-21
1 Tim 3:1-13
1 Tim 4:13-14
1 Tim 5:17-22
2 Tim 2:1-2
Titus 1:5-9

III. DOCTRINES

---

8. Love One Another

"If you love me, you will keep my commandments" (Jn 14:15).

Charity unites all the members of the Body of Christ (Rom 12:3-9).

Mt 5:43-45
Mt 19:19
Mt 22:36-40
Mt 25:31-46
Mk 12:28-34
Lk 6:27-36
Jn 13:34-35
Jn 15:12-17
Rom 10:1
Rom 12:9-13
Rom 15:30-32
1 Cor 10:24
1 Cor 13
Gal 5:9-13, 6:2

1 Thess 3:12; 4:9-10, 18
1 Thess 5:11, 14-15
1 Tim 2:1-4
1 Jn 4:7-21
Jas 2:14-17

9. There is Only One God

Deut 6:4-5
Is 40:25-28
Is 41:4
Is 43:10-13
Is 44:6-8
1 Chron 17:20
Mk 12:29
1 Cor 8:4-6

10. The Holy Spirit is God

Jn 14:16-17
Jn 14:25-26
Acts 5:3-4
Acts 13:2-4
Acts 15:28-29
Acts 21:11

11. Jesus Christ is True God

> Deut 5:11
>
> Mt 2:1-11 (The Wise Men "worship" the Christ Child)
>
> Mt 4:10-11, Lk 4:8, Acts 10:25-26 (Worship God alone!)
>
> Jn 1:1-18
>
> Jn 8:23-30
>
> Jn 8:52-59 ("So they took up stones to throw at him because they understood that he claimed to be God [I AM]"; Ex 20:7)
>
> Jn 10:24-42
>
> Jn 20:26-28 ("My lord and my God")
>
> Col 1:15-20
>
> Titus 2:11-14

12. The Trinity

Old Testament "theophany" (mysterious appearance/reference to one or more persons of the Trinity): Is 7:14 (Emmanuel means "God is with us"), 9:6, 11:2, 35:4; Prov 8:22-31; Mal 3:1

> Mt 3:16-17
>
> Mt 28:18-19

Jn 10:38
Jn 14:9 –21, 26
Jn 17:10
1 Tim 2:5

13. The Saints: Their Glory, Example, and Intercession

Rom 2:9
Phil 3:17-20
1 Thess 1:6-7
2 Thess 3:7
Heb 12:1

14. Life After Death: Heaven and Hell

Is 33:11-14
Mt 8:11-12
Mt 25:41-43
Mk 9:41-48
Lk 3:17
1 Cor 13:12
2 Cor 12:1-4
2 Thess 1:9
Phil 3:20-21
Rev 14:11
Rev 21 & 22

15. The Blessed Virgin Mary

Mary is prefigured in the Old Testament in the form of various "types" or foreshadowings (Gen 3:15; Heb 9:24; 2 Mac 7:20-23).

Christ is the second Adam (Rom 5:14) and took his flesh from Mary; prefigured by the Ark of the Covenant that carried within itself the Word of God in Scripture (Mary carried in her womb the Word of God in flesh), Solomon's Temple, and the Ark that saved Noah and his family from the great flood.

Mary, the Mother of God (Greek: theotokos = *"God bearer")*

> Mt 1:18-25
> Mt 2:10-11
> Lk 1:41-44
> Gal 4:4

Mary's Immaculate Conception

> Her Immaculate Conception was the perfect fulfillment of several imperfect Old Tes-

tament types (i.e., Foreshadowing; Heb 1:1; Col 2:17; 1 Cor 15:15-47)

Lk 1:26-35, 39-43

Mary foreshadowed by the Ark of the Covenant (Lk 1)

Ex 25:10-16

Lk 1:38-41, 56

Mary's Bodily Assumption into Heaven

Not mentioned in Scripture. However, other bodily "assumptions" are mentioned — Enoch (Gen 5:24; Heb 11:5), Elijah (2 Kings 2:1, 11-12), and those alive at the second coming (1 Thess 4:13-18).

Rev 12: 1-8

Mary's Perpetual Virginity

The "brothers of the Lord" (Mt 12:46-48; 13:55-56; 27:56)

Lk 1:34 suggests Mary had made a vow of perpetual virginity to God.

Lk 2:41-51, "Finding in the Temple" — no other children mentioned.

Jn 7:3-4 — the "brothers" (ie disciples) of Christ, who did not believe in him, give him rather forceful advice. This type of exchange from younger brothers to the oldest brother would have been highly unusual and disrespectful.

Jn 19 — Christ entrusted his mother to the Apostle John, a man outside the family.

Mt 1:25 sometimes is used as a "firstborn" argument, i.e., the first of many children. But the term "firstborn" applies both as a title of honor (Gen 43:33-34, even for a younger son) and to the biological fact of being the oldest child (see also below, re: use of "until").

Mt 13:55-56 — Four men are named as the "brothers of the Lord." However, at least two of them (James and Joseph) were actually sons of Mary the wife of Cleophas (Mt 27:56, Jn 19:25), and so not actually Jesus' literal "brothers."

Lk 1:29-31

Mt 1:25 — He knew her not *until* she had brought forth her firstborn son.

Note: Words for "until," *heos hou* **and** *heos,* **are an abbreviation of** *"heos hou chronou en hoi"* **=**

"until the time when." Both *heos* and the longer *heos hou* mean the same thing: "until." But, unlike our English "until," they don't necessarily indicate that a condition changes in the clause following the word "until."

Examples of this usage:

Ps 111:8 (Septuagint Version)

Acts 25:21 (where St Paul was ordered to be remanded into custody **until** [*heos hou*] he was sent to Caesar. But Acts shows that he was kept in custody even *after* that had occurred.

In 2 Pet 1:19, St. Peter tells Christians they should be attentive to God's Word **until** the "day dawns and the morning star rises in your hearts." Clearly, however, even once the morning star rises in our hearts, we won't forget about God's Word.

Mt 28:20 — Christ says, "I will be with you until the end of the world." He will be with his people *after* the end of the world, too.

1 Cor 15:25 — Christ will reign as king until he has put all his enemies under his feet. He will reign as king *after* that point, as well.

1 Tim 4:13 — "Attend to teaching . . . **until** I arrive." Timothy would continue teaching *after* St Paul's arrival.

Mary needed a Savior.

Lk 1:46-49

Mary's sinlessness did not mean that she did not need Christ as her Savior; she herself proclaimed Him to be such. Christ indeed saved Mary from sin — from all sin — but he did this for her *prior* to her contracting sin. We, on the other hand, are saved *after* we fall into it.

16. Original Sin

Gen 2:15-17
Gen 3:8-19
Is 43:27
Rom 5:12-19
1 Cor 15:21-22
Eph 2:1-3

17. Purgatory

2 Mac 12:42-46
Mt 12:32

Lk 12:58
Lk 16:19-31
1 Cor 3:10-15
1 Pet 3:19
Rev 21:27

18. Salvation

Mt 7:21-23
Mt 19:16-17
Mt 24:13
Mt 25:34-36
Lk 6:46-49
Rom 2:3-8
Rom 2:13
Rom 5:2
Rom 11:22-23
Gal 5:5-6
Eph 2:8-9
Phil 2:12-13
Heb 10:24-31
2 Pet 2:20-21
1 Jn 3:7; 5:3

19. Grace

Infused Grace (i.e., "poured into the soul," the soul is "filled" with God's grace)

> Acts 2:17-18
> Acts 4:31
> Acts 6:8
> Rom 1:5
> Titus 3:5-7

Grace is lost through mortal sin (1 Jn 5:16-17).

> Rom 11:21-22
> Heb 10: 26-31
> 2 Pet 2:20-22

The bad works of sin bring about eternal death: hell.

> Mt 25:31-46
> Rom 2:1-13
> 1 Cor 6:9-11
> 1 Cor 10:6-13
> 2 Cor 5:9-10
> Gal 5:13-21
> Gal 6:6-10
> Rev 22:12-15

IV. THE SACRAMENTS

20. Sacraments in General

Gen 1:31 — God loves matter ("It is very good.")
Mt 26:26-28
Mk 6:13
Mk 8:22-26
Jn 3:3-7, 22
Titus 3:5
1 Pet 3:20-21
Jas 5:13-15

21. Baptism

Necessity and effects of

Mt 28:19
Mk 16:15-16
Jn 3:4-5, 22
Acts 16:30-33
Acts 22:16
Rom 6:2-4
Titus 3:3-7

22. Infant Baptism

Acts 2:37-4 — "Repent and be baptized . . . this promise is made to you *and to your children.*"

Gen 17:1-14 — Circumcision was the normative way to bring a male child into the Covenant.

Col 2:11-15 — Baptism replaces circumcision. Jewish parents covenanted with God, on behalf of their infant son, through circumcision; now, Christian parents covenant with God, on behalf of their infant children, through baptism.

God bestows blessings or forgiveness or healing on one person because of the faith and spiritual diligence of another person.

Gen 18:16-33
Mt 8:5-13
Mt 15:21-28
Lk 7:1-20
Lk 18:15-17

"Whole families" or *"entire households"* were baptized (which almost certainly included children).

Acts 16:15
Acts 16:27-33

23. Confession of Sins to a Priest

Mt 9:1-8
Mt 10:40
Mt 18:18-19
Mk 2:5-12
Jn 20:22-23
2 Cor 5:18-20
Lk 10:16
Jas 5:16
1 Jn 1:6-9

24. Mortal and Venial Sins

1 Jn 5:16-17

25. The Holy Eucharist

Ex 12:21-28 Passover Lamb
Mt 26: 26-28
Mk 14:22-25
Lk 22:14-20

Jn 1:28-30 (Jesus is "the Lamb of God Who takes away the sins of the world")
Jn 6:35-58
1 Cor 10:16
1 Cor 11:23-29

26. The Priesthood (Holy Orders)

Rom 12:4 — "members [of the Body of Christ] do not all have the same function."

Christ shares his sacred ministries with others.

Christ is the shepherd of His flock, the Church (Jn 10:16), but he conferred that role, in a subordinate way, on his Apostles and on others (Jn 21:15-17; Eph 4:11; 1 Pet 5:1-4).

Christ is the supreme king of the universe (1 Tim 1:17, 6:15-17; Rev 17:14, 19:16), but those in heaven share in his kingship, wear crowns, sit on thrones, and reign as kings alongside Christ (Rev 4:4,10).

Christ is the supreme judge (Jn 5:27-28, 9:39; 2 Cor 5:10;), but Christians will judge the angels (Mt 19:28; Lk 22:28-30; 1 Cor 6:2-3).

Christ is the "High priest of the New Covenant," eternally present before the Father, offering His redemptive sacrifice (Heb 3:1,5:1-10,7:15-26, 9:11-12).

All Christians receive a share in Christ's priesthood (1 Pet 2:4-5, 9; Rev 1:6, 5:10, 20:6).

Num 18:6-7 — God establishes a special sacrificial priesthood among the people.

Mt 10:1, 16:16-19
Lk 10:16
1 Thess 5:12
1 Tim 4:14 , 5:22
2 Tim 1:6
Titus 1:5
Jas 3:1

V. CUSTOMS AND PRACTICES

27. Call No Man "Father"

Mt 23:1-12: also says call no man "master" or "teacher." However, the word "doctor" is also a Latin word for "teacher." Therefore, if Catholics are "unbiblical" for calling priests "father," Protestant ministers who have the title "doctor" are similarly unbiblical.

    Acts 7:2
    Acts 7:38-39
    Acts 7:44-45
    Acts 21:40
    Acts 22:1
    Rom 4:16-17
    1 Cor 4:14-15
    1 Thess 2:11
    1 Tim 1:2
    Titus 1:4
    Philem 1:10

1 Jn 2:13-14

28. Necessity of Suffering and the Possibility of Persecution

Mt 5:11-12
Mt 10:16-28
Rom 8:14-18
Col 1:24-26
Phil 1:27-30
Heb 11:32-40
Heb 12:5-6
1 Pet 1:6-7
1 Pet 2:18-24
1 Pet 3:13-17
1 Pet 4:1

29. Priestly Celibacy

Mt 19:10-12
1 Cor 7:32-35
Rev 14:3-4

30. Crucifixes

Mt 16:24
Lk 23:38
1 Cor 2:1-2

1 Cor 1:18-24
Gal 2:20, 3:1, 5:24, 6:14
Eph 2:13-17
Col 1:19-20

31. Relics

2 Kings 13:20-21
Ps 116:15
Mt 14:34-36
Mk 6:56
Lk 8:40-43
Acts 5:14-16
Acts 19:11-12

32. Statues, Graven Images, and the Sin of Idolatry

Idolatry condemned

Ex 20:3-5
Deut 5:6-9
Deut 7:5, 25, 9:12, 12:3
Deut 27:15
Num 33:52
2 Kings 17:9-18, 23:24
2 Chron 23:17, 28:1-3, 22:18-25, 34:1-7

Rom 1:18-23
1 Cor 10:14

Statues not condemned per se:

Ex 25:18-20, 22
Num 21:8-9
1 Sam 6:1-18
1 Kings 3:1-28
1 Kings 6:23-35
1 Kings 9:3
2 Kings 18:4
Jn 3:14; 8:28; 14:9
Col 1:15

33. Tithing

1 Cor 16:1-2
2 Cor 9:5-14

34. Vain Repetition

Ps 136 — the beauty of a repetitive refrain in
   prayer
Dan 3: 57-88
Mt 6:7
Mt 26:39, 42, 44
Rev 4:8-11

35. Wine and Strong Drink

God condemns the abuse *of alcohol* — *"drunken-ness."*

Prov 20:1
Prov 23:21
Habakkuk 2:15
Is 5:11
Eph 5:18

God does not condemn the drinking *of alcohol.*

Deut 14:26
Eccl 10:19
Ps 104:15
Jn 2:1-11
1 Tim 5:23

VI. MORAL ISSUES

36. Abortion

Is 49: 1,5
Is 44:2, 24
Eccl 11:5
Jer 1:5
Wis 7:1-3
Sir 49:7
Lk 1:39-44

37. Divorce and Remarriage

Mal 2:16
Mt 5:31-32
Mt 19:3-10
Mt 19:16-19
Mk 10:11-12
Lk 16:18
Rom 7:2-3
1 Cor 7:10-11

38. Command to Love One Another

Jn 13:34-35
Jn 15:12-17
Rom 12:9-13
Gal 6:2
Eph 4:32
1 Thess 3:12; 4:9

39. Homosexuality

Gen 19:1-14
Lev 18:22
1 Cor 6:9-10
1 Tim 1:10

MORAL ISSUES

VII. NON-CATHOLIC BELIEFS

40. The Great Apostasy Theory (Mormonism)

Some passages Mormons cite:

> Acts 20:29-30
> 2 Thess 2:1-3
> Rev 13:7
> Mt 7:24-29 (Mt 16:18-19)

But in Mt 12:29, Christ is the "strong man" who guards his house, the Church (1 Tim 3:15). Satan cannot bind him and plunder the Church.

If there was a "total apostasy of the Church," as Mormons claim, then Christ was not only a liar for promising his permanent presence and protection for the Church, as he does in Lk 14:27-30, but he (and writers of Scripture) would also have been worse than foolish for saying things like this:

> Is 9:6-7
> Dan 2:44-45

Dan 7:13-14
Mt 16:18-19
Mk 3:27
Mt 28:18-20
Jn 14:15-20
1 Cor 11:26
2 Tim 4:2-4
2 Pet 2:1-2

41. "Inquisitions"

Deut 17:2-7
Num 25:1-7
Mt 10:12-15
Mt 18:15-18

42. Sabbath or Sunday Worship? (Seventh-Day Adventists)

Ex 20: 8-11
Jn 20:1 Christ rose from the dead on Sunday

Jesus has authority over the Sabbath.

Mt 12:8

Jesus gave this authority to His apostles and His Church.

> Mt 10:40
> Mt 16:19
> Mt 18:18-20
> Mt 28:1-6

43. The 144,000 (Jehovah's Witnesses)

Rev 7:1-9 — Jehovah's Witnesses claim only 144,000 people will be in heaven for eternity. Notice, however, that this group is identified as male virgins (Rev 14), while Jehovah's Witnesses don't believe in consecrated celibacy.

The 144,000 is a symbolic number (much of what is presented in the Book of Revelation is symbolic); it doesn't mean that only that specific number will be in heaven.

All Christians who are faithful to Christ will go to heaven.

> 1 Jn 3:2
> 1 Thess 4:13-18
> Phil 3:20-21
> Rom 8:16-17

44. Blood Transfusions (Jehovah's Witnesses)

Deut 12:23-25
Gen 9:3-4
Acts 15:28-29
Mk 7:19
Jn 6:52-53
1 Cor 6:12-13
Titus 1:14-16

45. Annihilation of Soul (Various Groups)

Mt 10:28
Rev 6:9-10
1 Sam 28:1-19
Mt 17:1-8
Lk 16

46. The Rapture

The most common version of this theory: Jesus will return in a hidden, silent way, to take up to heaven all "born-again Christians" just prior to the "Great Tribulation" period, during which the Anti-Christ (Mt 24:12) and the Beast (Rev 13-17) appear.